THE COCKTAIL CONNOISSEUR'S
RECIPE BOOK

◊ LOUISE ZEDDA-SAMPSON ◊

Important note

Some recipes in this book contain raw egg. People who might be at risk of salmonella poisoning (such as the elderly, those who are pregnant, young children – if these recipes are used as a base for mocktails – and those who are suffering from conditions that result in immune deficiency) or anyone who has concerns will need to consult their doctor about eating raw egg.

The Cocktail Connoisseur's Recipe Book

LZS Press
www.LZSPress.com.au

First published in 2024
Copyright text and images © Louise Zedda-Sampson

ISBN: 978-0-6451255-2-8

Author photo: Robyn Slavin

 A catalogue record for this book is available from the National Library of Australia

To Paul Sampson, for being there for the very looong cocktail-making and -creating journey, and for all the shared day afters.

Introduction	6
Standard drinks and measurements	7
Conversion charts	8
Making cocktails	10
Cocktail-making terminology	11
Types of glasses	12
It's all in the styling	13
Raw eggs and egg white alternatives	14
Syrups, aquafaba and rims	15
Cocktails	**19**
Drink finder	91
Acknowledgements	94

COCKTAILS

Absinthe Drip	20
Air Mail	21
Aperol Spritz	22
Astral Plane	23
Baby Guinness	24
Bee's Knees	25
Bellini	26
Between the Sheets	27
Black Russian	28
Bloody Mary	29
Bramble	30
Brandy Alexander	31
Breakfast Martini	32
Champagne Cocktail	33
Comfortably Numb	34
Corpse Reviver	35
Death by Chocolate	36
El Diablo	37
El Presidente	38
Esse Emme	39
Eternal Spirit	40
Eye Opener	41

Fluffy Duck	42
French 75	43
Fuzzy Navel	44
Gin and Tonic	45
Gin Basil Smash	46
Godfather	47
Godmother	48
Grasshopper	49
Green Goddess	50
Green With Envy	51
Hanky Panky	52
High Voltage	53
Honey Bee	54
Irish Coffee	55
Jungle Juice	56
Kir Royale	57
Lemon Drop	58
Love Potion #9	59
Margarita	60
Midori Sour	61
Mojito	62
Mudslide	63
Mulled Wine	64
Naked and Famous	66
Nutty Summer	67
Old Fashioned	68
Paloma	69
Perfect Storm	70
Piña Colada	71
Porn Star Martini	72
Quarantini	73
Rusty Nail	74
Sangria	75
Screwdriver	76
Sex on the Beach	77
Sidecar	78
Six Cylinder	79
Suffering Bastard	80
Sunflower	81
Swamp Thing	82
Tequila Sunrise	83
Tequila Sunset	84
Violet Fizz	85
Whiskey Sour	86
White Russian	87
Whoa, Nellie!	88
Woo Woo	89
Zombie	90

INTRODUCTION

The Cocktail Connoisseur's Recipe Book features the recipes for the 70 cocktails that appear on *The Cocktail Connoisseur's Message Cards*. It can be used in conjunction with the cards – for example, use the cards to select which cocktail you wish to make – or as a stand-alone recipe book.

Each cocktail has an image of the finished product and step-by-step directions on how to make it and even what glass to use. The book also includes the basic techniques you can use to make your cocktails look as divine as they taste, and tips on how to garnish. You will find recipes for syrups and also a metric-to-imperial conversion chart if you need it.

The recipes come from a variety of sources, including cocktail books (from the early 20th century to the present day) and recipes freely available on the internet. Some of them you may already know, or you may create them with slightly different ingredients or measures. Historically, cocktails have been added to and changed over time, which is why it's often impossible to find a 'standard' or original version.

However you make and shake them, I hope this book and the cocktails within bring you enjoyment.

From my glass to yours (clink).

Cheers!
Louise

STANDARD DRINKS AND MEASUREMENTS

The standard drink size varies depending on where you live. This book contains Australian standard drink measures. All the recipes in this book are a minimum of one standard Australian drink.

One Australian standard drink is equal to approximately:

- 285 ml full-strength beer (4.6% alc. vol.)
- 425 ml low-strength beer (2.7% alc. vol.)
- 255 ml cider (5% alc. vol.)
- 100 ml wine or Champagne (12% alc. vol.)
- 30 ml spirits (40% alc. vol.)

The measurements in the book are Australian and metric. Please refer to the conversion charts on pages 8–9 if you wish to convert to imperial measurements, or to check standard measurements for teaspoons and tablespoons.

Drink responsibly

While these cocktails may look pretty and inviting, they will knock you right out – some are four-drinks strong. Drinking can be all fun and games until someone gets alcohol poisoning or experiences alcohol-related trauma.

Think of yourself and your family and friends, and please drink responsibly. In Australia, the Alcohol and Drug Foundation is one organisation of many that offers support and information for people affected by alcohol and drug use. Please contact your local support services if you are affected.

CONVERSION CHARTS

Converting metric to imperial for small and half measures often results in ounces with up to five decimal places, so measurements have been rounded in the tables below for simplicity and ease of measuring. The measurements in the book are Australian and metric.

Centimetres to inches

centimetre	inch
1	0.4

Spoon measurements

ml	spoon
1.25 ml	1/4 teaspoon
2.5 ml	1/2 teaspoon
5 ml	1 teaspoon
20 ml	1 tablespoon

Weight

Metric	Imperial
200 g	7 oz
250 g	9 oz
300 g	10 1/2 oz
425 g	15 oz

Volume

Metric	Imperial
2.5 ml	1/10 fl oz
5 ml	1/5 fl oz
7.5 ml	1/4 fl oz
10 ml	1/3 fl oz
12.5 ml	5/12 fl oz
15 ml	1/2 fl oz
20 ml	2/3 fl oz
22.5 ml	3/4 fl oz
30 ml	1 fl oz
37.5 ml	1 1/4 fl oz
40 ml	1 1/3 fl oz
45 ml	1 1/2 fl oz
50 ml	1 2/3 fl oz
52.5 ml	1 3/4 fl oz
60 ml	2 fl oz
70 ml	2 1/3 fl oz

Metric	Imperial
75 ml	2 1/2 fl oz
80 ml	2 2/3 fl oz
90 ml	3 fl oz
120 ml	4 fl oz
125 ml	4 1/5 fl oz
135 ml	4 1/2 fl oz
150 ml	5 fl oz
180 ml	6 fl oz
185 ml	6 1/5 fl oz
200 ml	6 2/3 fl oz
210 ml	7 fl oz
225 ml	7 1/2 fl oz
240 ml	8 fl oz

MAKING COCKTAILS

You're probably keen to start making and shaking, but I promise reading through this section will save you time and heartache later. A few tips before you start:

- A good shake lasts 20–30 seconds, so be prepared to work those arms if you are having a party!
- Always use fresh fruit and freshly squeezed fruit juices where you can – the flavour is always better. Tomato juice, however, is best canned.
- Remember that cocktails are often 2–3 standard drinks each.
- Read the warning about raw eggs.

Have fun! Use the recipe book to get ideas, then make some cocktails to call your own. You are the mixologist!

COCKTAIL-MAKING TERMINOLOGY

If you are new to cocktail-making, there may be unfamiliar terms in the instructions. Here are those that are relevant to cocktail preparation.

Churn: Stir ingredients with crushed ice.

Float: Pour alcohol over the back of a spoon so the alcohol 'floats' evenly on top of the cocktail. You can do the same with cream, although pouring seems to suffice here.

Layer: Mainly called for in shots but can apply to other cocktails as well. Layering can be tricky to do successfully, so use whatever works, be it pouring over the back of a spoon or using a syringe.

Muddle: Usually applied to something like mint leaves or soft fruits, where the ingredient is lightly bruised to release the flavours.

Shake: This one's a no-brainer! Combine ingredients in a cocktail shaker with ice and shake until the shaker feels cold on the outside.

Strain: Many cocktails are served without ice or the ingredients they were muddled with, and are required to be strained before serving. A shaker can have an inbuilt strainer, or you may need a separate one.

Stir: Some cocktails are not shaken but stirred. Stirring is a less violent action than shaking, so the dilution and chilling of the drink is reduced. Pour the drink directly into the glass over ice and stir for about 20 seconds until the ice starts to melt. The length of time a drink is stirred for can vary – it basically boils down to bartender and/or consumer preference.

TYPES OF GLASSES

Most cocktails are historically served in a particular type of glass. If a recipe lists 'cocktail' as the glass type, it means you can choose a coupe, a martini or a Nick and Nora glass. However, the rules are your own when it comes to creating, and you can use whatever glass you choose.

As you'll see, some images in this book depict different glasses than those suggested in the recipe. Generally, if the cocktail is served with ice it's in a short glass like a lowball or old-fashioned or a tall one like a highball or a Collins, and if it's strained it's usually in a cocktail glass.

IT'S ALL IN THE STYLING

You can jazz up your cocktails with simple tricks. Umbrellas are great ... but have we moved on? Aside from a Tequila Sunrise, I think so! Citrus fruits can be cut into wedges or slices (to look like wheels) or formed into a twist. Peel can be shaped to form a twist on the side of the glass, or gently squeezed into the cocktail to add a bit of bite and colour. Pineapple chunks look great when matched with a cherry on a hurricane glass. Don't forget cherries – maraschino or brandied cherries look (and taste) great and can be used for lots of cocktails. Chocolate can be grated, and cinnamon can be sprinkled. And then there are the sweet sugar rims . . .

Chocolate swirls

For chocolatey drinks, add extra chocolate to the glass. It emphasises the chocolate taste and looks great as well. Will people think you are as skilled as Tom Cruise's character in the 1988 movie Cocktail? Maybe.

To make a chocolate swirl, simply squirt chocolate topping around the glass before serving the cocktail. This works best if the glass is well chilled.

Edible glitter

My word, yes, cocktail glitter is a thing! There are glitters and shimmers and sprays. Lots of products are available online, but check your local supermarket first just in case it has something you can use. Ensure a product is edible if you plan to use it in your cocktails.

Ice cubes and spheres

Ice can be a decoration. Consider using fun ice-cube trays or ice spheres and different shapes, or even freezing edible flowers.

Sugar rims

A sugar rim is a simple and effective way to spruce up a cocktail. The instruction for sugar rims is on page 17.

RAW EGGS AND EGG WHITE ALTERNATIVES

Egg whites

Many cocktails use egg whites to create foam and texture, but there is a risk when ingesting raw eggs (yolk and white) of salmonella poisoning. People who are elderly, pregnant, infants and immunocompromised are recommended not to ingest raw eggs. If choosing a recipe that contains raw egg, follow the directions about shaking carefully, and use pasteurised eggs where possible. Pasteurised egg whites can be purchased from your local supermarket.

Each cocktail recipe containing egg whites asks you to 'dry shake' the whites and other ingredients first without any ice. This ensures the egg white combines with the other ingredients and produces a smooth, frothy texture. This is also requested for recipes containing egg yolks as it will also thicken the mixture. The second shake is with ice to chill the cocktail.

By dry shaking the egg whites first, you change the structure of the protein in them in the same way as when you make meringues.

Egg white replacements

Egg white replacements can be found at the supermarket, or you can make a replacement called aquafaba from tinned chickpea liquid (see recipe on page 15). You can also use Wonderfoam, a vegan alternative available from major liquor merchants.

How much egg white (or replacement) to use

Use half a medium-sized egg white per cocktail. If using pre-packaged whites, use 15 ml, and if using aquafaba, 20 ml. If using Wonderfoam, follow the directions on the label.

SYRUPS, AQUAFABA AND RIMS

You can buy some syrups at your local supermarket or bottle shop, but some you will need to make yourself. I've included recipes for all syrups that appear in this book except agave syrup, which is available at the supermarket. Many of the syrups can also be used as a topping for ice-cream or desserts – so the excess doesn't have to go to waste.

AQUAFABA

Aquafaba is great as a vegan egg replacement, but it comes with a warning. The saponins in chickpea liquid don't agree with everyone as they can be difficult to digest. Please bear this in mind if you have food sensitivities. Aquafaba can be used for any egg white replacement.

Note: 2 tablespoons aquafaba = 1 egg white

Ingredients

1 400g can no added salt chickpeas

1/4 teaspoon cream of tartar

Method

Strain the chickpea liquid through a sieve and into a mixing bowl. Reserve the chickpeas to use later – or use them in a salad or a soup. Add cream of tartar and mix the liquid on low speed for 5–10 minutes until stiff peaks form. Use the day it is made, or store in a sealed container in the fridge for three days.

HONEY SYRUP

Ingredients

1/2 cup honey, any type
1/2 cup boiling water

Method

Combine honey and boiling water in a bowl or jug. Stir until the honey has dissolved. Cool completely before using. Store in the fridge for up to a week.

STRAWBERRY SYRUP

Ingredients

200 g caster sugar
225 ml water
2 cups fresh or frozen strawberries

Method

Place sugar and water in a small pan and bring to the boil. Once sugar has dissolved, add strawberries and simmer for 20-25 minutes. Strain through a sieve. Cool completely before using. Store in the fridge for up to a week.

SUGAR (AND SALT) RIMS

A plain or coloured rim is a simple and effective decoration.

Ingredients

1 tablespoon caster sugar (or salt)

food dye (optional)

lemon wedge

Method

Tip sugar onto a flat plate in a heap. Add a few drops of your desired food colouring (if using) and mix into sugar with a flat-bladed knife. Rub lemon wedge around the rim of your glass, then dip the glass into the sugar and set aside to dry. Alternatively, squeeze lemon wedge onto a flat plate, then dip the rim of the glass in the juice and then in the sugar. Set aside to dry.

Note: Some recipes, such as a Margarita, call for a salt rim. The method is the same.

SUGAR SYRUP

Ingredients

200 g caster sugar

100 ml water

Method

Place ingredients in a small pan over a low heat. Stir until sugar dissolves. Once the liquid starts to simmer, remove from heat and allow to cool before using. Store in the fridge for up to a week.

COCKTAILS

ABSINTHE DRIP

INGREDIENTS
45 ml absinthe
1 sugar cube
60 ml water

METHOD
Pour absinthe into an absinthe glass. Rest a slotted absinthe spoon over the glass and place sugar cube on top. Drip water over sugar cube so sugar dissolves and drips into glass. The absinthe will change colour to a milky white.

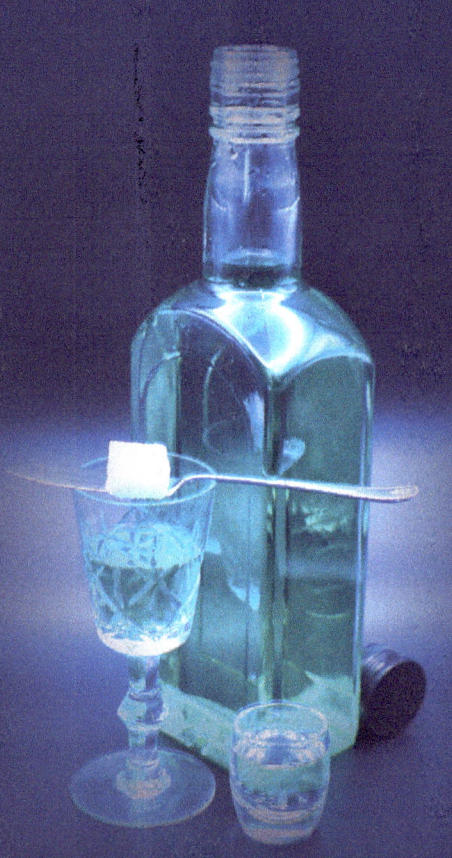

AIR MAIL

INGREDIENTS
30 ml gold rum
15 ml lime juice
15 ml honey syrup
25 ml soda water
Garnish: mint sprig

METHOD
Combine rum, lime juice and honey syrup in a cocktail shaker with ice. Shake until the outside of the cocktail shaker becomes frosted. Strain and pour into a highball glass filled with ice. Top with soda water. Garnish.

Note: The recipe for honey syrup is on page 16.

APEROL SPRITZ

INGREDIENTS
75 ml prosecco
50 ml Aperol
25 ml soda water
Garnish: orange slice

METHOD
Fill a wine glass with ice and pour in prosecco. Add Aperol, then top with soda water. Garnish.

ASTRAL PLANE

INGREDIENTS
30 ml white port
30 ml Salers Gentiane
30 ml lemon juice
22.5 ml sugar syrup
2 dashes Peychaud's Bitters
60 ml soda water
Garnish: lemon or grapefruit slice

METHOD
Combine white port, Salers Gentiane, lemon juice, sugar syrup and Peychaud's Bitters in a cocktail shaker with ice. Shake until the outside of the cocktail shaker becomes frosted. Strain and pour into a Collins glass filled with ice. Top with soda water. Garnish.

Note: The recipe for sugar syrup is on page 17.

BABY GUINNESS

Some preparation is required to make this cocktail.

INGREDIENTS
60 ml coffee liqueur
15 ml Irish cream

METHOD
Chill coffee liqueur and Irish cream overnight. Pour coffee liqueur into a chilled shot glass then, to layer, pour in Irish cream slowly over the back of a spoon.

BEE'S KNEES

INGREDIENTS
60 ml dry gin
30 ml lemon juice
15 ml honey syrup
Garnish: lemon twist

METHOD
Combine all ingredients in a cocktail shaker with ice. Shake until the outside of the cocktail shaker becomes frosted. Strain and pour into a cocktail glass. Garnish.

Note 1: The recipe for honey syrup is on page 16.

Note 2: A variation to this recipe is to reduce the lemon juice to 20 ml and add 10 ml orange juice.

BELLINI

INGREDIENTS

2 fresh peaches or 8 pieces tinned peach slices
150 ml prosecco
Garnish: peach slice

METHOD

Puree peaches, then pour 30 ml peach puree directly into a champagne flute. Top with prosecco and stir gently before serving. Garnish.

BETWEEN THE SHEETS

INGREDIENTS
30 ml white rum
30 ml cognac
30 ml triple sec
15 ml lemon juice
Garnish: lemon peel

METHOD
Combine all ingredients in a cocktail shaker with ice. Shake until the outside of the cocktail shaker becomes frosted. Strain and pour into a cocktail glass. Garnish.

BLACK RUSSIAN

INGREDIENTS

45 ml Kahlúa

45 ml vodka

METHOD

Fill an old-fashioned glass with ice, then pour in Kahlúa and vodka. Stir.

BLOODY MARY

INGREDIENTS
125 ml canned tomato juice
60 ml vodka
15 ml lemon juice
2 dashes Tabasco sauce
2 dashes Worcestershire sauce
salt and black pepper, to taste
Garnish: celery stick

METHOD
Fill a Collins glass with ice. Add ingredients in the above order. Stir. Garnish.

BRAMBLE

INGREDIENTS
45 ml gin
30 ml lemon juice
15 ml sugar syrup
15 ml Crème de Mûre
Garnish: blackberries or lemon wedge

METHOD
Combine gin, lemon juice and sugar syrup in a cocktail shaker with ice. Shake until the outside of the cocktail shaker becomes frosted. Strain and pour into an old-fashioned glass filled with ice. Pour Crème de Mûre over ice in centre. Garnish.

Note: The recipe for sugar syrup is on page 17.

BRANDY ALEXANDER

INGREDIENTS

45 ml brandy

30 ml crème de cacao

30 ml cream

Garnish: sprinkle of ground nutmeg or cinnamon

METHOD

Combine all ingredients in a cocktail shaker with ice. Shake until the outside of the cocktail shaker becomes frosted. Strain and pour into a cocktail glass. Garnish.

BREAKFAST MARTINI

INGREDIENTS
50 ml dry gin
15 ml Cointreau
15 ml lemon juice
1 teaspoon orange marmalade
Garnish: orange twist

METHOD
Combine all ingredients in a cocktail shaker with ice. Shake until the outside of the cocktail shaker becomes frosted. Strain and pour into a martini glass. Garnish.

CHAMPAGNE COCKTAIL

INGREDIENTS
1 sugar cube
3 dashes bitters
10 ml cognac
75 ml Champagne
Garnish: orange peel (optional)

METHOD
Place sugar cube on a small dish and drizzle with bitters, turning the cube a few times to coat. Drop cube into a champagne flute, pour in cognac, then slowly top with Champagne. Twist orange peel into the flute to express the juices, then use as a garnish or discard.

COMFORTABLY NUMB

INGREDIENTS
absinthe, to rinse
45 ml Southern Comfort
15 ml Cointreau
7.5 ml pimento dram
30 ml pear puree
Garnish: 2 dashes falernum bitters

METHOD
Rinse the inside of a lowball glass with absinthe, then discard the excess. Fill the glass with ice and set aside. Combine remaining ingredients in a cocktail shaker with ice. Shake until the outside of the cocktail shaker becomes frosted. Strain and pour into glass. Garnish.

CORPSE REVIVER

INGREDIENTS
30 ml cognac
30 ml Calvados
15 ml sweet vermouth
Garnish: lemon or orange twist

METHOD
Put all ingredients in a mixing glass with ice and stir until well chilled. Strain and pour into a cocktail glass. Garnish.

DEATH BY CHOCOLATE

INGREDIENTS
chocolate topping
60 ml chocolate liqueur
30 ml vodka
30 ml cream
Garnish: Lindor ball on skewer

METHOD
Chill a cocktail glass in the fridge for at least 15 minutes, then swirl chocolate topping inside it to create a pattern. Return glass to the fridge. Combine chocolate liqueur, vodka and cream in a cocktail shaker with ice. Shake until the outside of the cocktail shaker becomes frosted. Strain and pour into the prepared glass. Garnish.

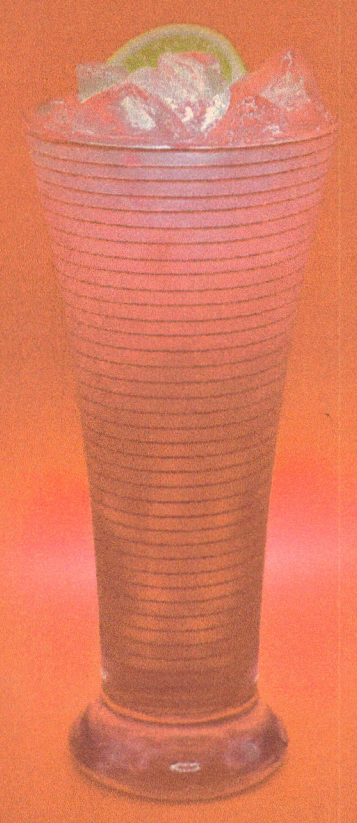

EL DIABLO

INGREDIENTS
45 ml tequila
15 ml crème de cassis
15 ml lime juice
120 ml ginger beer
Garnish: lime wedge or peel

METHOD
Combine tequila, crème de cassis and lime juice in a cocktail shaker with ice. Shake until the outside of the cocktail shaker becomes frosted. Strain and pour into a Collins glass filled with ice. Top with ginger beer. Garnish.

EL PRESIDENTE

INGREDIENTS
45 ml white rum
22.5 ml dry vermouth
7.5 ml orange curaçao
2 dashes grenadine
Garnish: orange twist

METHOD
Add all ingredients to a mixing glass with ice and stir until well chilled. Strain and pour into a Collins glass. Garnish.

ESSE EMME

INGREDIENTS

30 ml Grey Goose vodka
30 ml parfait d'amour
10 ml peach schnapps
5 ml blue curaçao
4 drops strawberry syrup
20 ml cream, to float

METHOD

Combine vodka, parfait d'amour, peach schnapps, blue curaçao and strawberry syrup in a cocktail shaker with ice. Shake until the outside of the cocktail shaker becomes frosted. Strain and pour into a cocktail glass. Float cream on top.

Note: The recipe for strawberry syrup is on page 16.

ETERNAL SPIRIT

INGREDIENTS

45 ml Bacardi Carta Blanca
15 ml Bianco vermouth
10 ml amaretto
20 ml lemon juice
1 teaspoon icing sugar
3 slices cucumber, 1 cm thick, peeled
Garnish: lemon peel

METHOD

Combine all ingredients in a cocktail shaker with ice. Shake until the outside of the cocktail shaker becomes frosted. Strain and pour into a cocktail glass. Garnish.

EYE OPENER

INGREDIENTS
45 ml rum
5 ml absinthe
5 ml orange curaçao
5 ml amaretto
1 teaspoon icing sugar
1 egg yolk
Garnish: orange twist

METHOD
Combine all ingredients in a cocktail shaker without ice (shaking without ice changes the egg yolk consistency). Add ice and shake again until the outside of the cocktail shaker becomes frosted. Strain and pour into an old-fashioned glass filled with ice. Garnish.

FLUFFY DUCK

INGREDIENTS
30 ml gin
30 ml advocaat
20 ml triple sec
20 ml orange juice
30 ml soda water
Garnish: orange slice

METHOD
Combine gin, advocaat, triple sec and orange juice in a cocktail shaker with ice. Shake until the outside of the cocktail shaker becomes frosted. Strain and pour into a hurricane glass. Top with soda water. Garnish.

Note: For a Rum Fluffy Duck, replace the gin with rum and replace the soda water with lemonade, and add 30 ml cream.

FRENCH 75

INGREDIENTS
45 ml gin
22.5 ml lemon juice
22.5 ml sugar syrup
90 ml sparkling wine
Garnish: lemon peel

METHOD
Combine gin, lemon juice and sugar syrup in a cocktail shaker with ice. Shake until the outside of the cocktail shaker becomes frosted. Strain and pour into a cocktail glass. Top with sparkling wine. Garnish.

Note: The recipe for sugar syrup is on page 17.

FUZZY NAVEL

INGREDIENTS

60 ml peach schnapps
120 ml orange juice
Garnish: peach slice or orange twist

METHOD

Fill a Collins glass with ice. Add peach schnapps and then orange juice. Garnish.

Note: To make a Hairy Navel, replace 30 ml of the peach schnapps with 30 ml vodka.

GIN AND TONIC

INGREDIENTS
60 ml gin
120 ml tonic water
Garnish: lime slice

METHOD
Fill an old-fashioned glass with ice. Add gin and then tonic water. Stir. Garnish.

GIN BASIL SMASH

INGREDIENTS

a few sprigs of basil
50 ml gin
25 ml lemon juice
15 ml sugar syrup
Garnish: lemon wedge and basil sprigs

METHOD

In a cocktail shaker, muddle basil sprigs to extract juice. Add remaining ingredients with ice. Shake until the outside of the cocktail shaker becomes frosted. Strain and pour into an old-fashioned glass. Garnish.

Note: The recipe for sugar syrup is on page 17.

GODFATHER

INGREDIENTS
60 ml Scotch whisky
60 ml amaretto
Garnish: orange peel and brandied cherry

METHOD
Pour whisky and amaretto in any order into an old-fashioned glass filled with ice. Stir and garnish.

GODMOTHER

INGREDIENTS
45 ml vodka
30 ml amaretto
Garnish: orange peel and brandied cherry

METHOD
Pour vodka and amaretto in any order into an old-fashioned glass filled with ice. Stir and garnish.

GRASSHOPPER

INGREDIENTS
30 ml crème de menthe
30 ml white crème de cacao
30 ml cream
Garnish: mint leaves

METHOD
Combine all ingredients in a cocktail shaker with ice. Shake until the outside of the cocktail shaker becomes frosted. Strain and pour into a cocktail glass. Garnish.

GREEN GODDESS

INGREDIENTS
½ kiwifruit, peeled
60 ml gin
22.5 ml elderflower liqueur
30 ml sugar syrup
15 ml lime juice
soda water, to top
Garnish: kiwifruit slice

METHOD
In a cocktail shaker, muddle kiwifruit to yield as much juice as possible. Add gin, elderflower liqueur, sugar syrup and lime juice and shake until the outside of the cocktail shaker becomes frosted. Strain and pour into a cocktail glass. Top with soda water. Garnish.

Note: The recipe for sugar syrup is on page 17.

GREEN WITH ENVY

INGREDIENTS

3 slices cucumber, 1 cm thick, peeled
10 g rocket (arugula)
60 ml gin
7.5 ml green Chartreuse
30 ml lime juice
15 ml sugar syrup

METHOD

In a cocktail shaker, muddle cucumber slices to yield as much juice as possible. Add rocket and muddle it as well. Add remaining ingredients with ice and shake until the outside of the cocktail shaker becomes frosted. Strain and pour into a cocktail glass.

Note: The recipe for sugar syrup is on page 17.

HANKY PANKY

INGREDIENTS
40 ml dry gin
40 ml sweet vermouth
5 ml Fernet-Branca
Garnish: orange twist

METHOD
Combine all ingredients in a mixing glass filled with ice. Stir. Strain and pour into a cocktail glass. Garnish.

HIGH VOLTAGE

INGREDIENTS
90 ml tequila
30 ml peach schnapps
22.5 ml lime juice

METHOD
Combine all ingredients in a cocktail shaker with ice. Shake until the outside of the cocktail shaker becomes frosted. Strain and pour into a cocktail glass.

HONEY BEE

INGREDIENTS
60 ml aged rum
30 ml lemon juice
15 ml honey syrup
Garnish: lemon twist

METHOD
Combine all ingredients in a cocktail shaker with ice. Shake until the outside of the cocktail shaker becomes frosted. Strain and pour into a cocktail glass. Garnish.

Note: The recipe for honey syrup is on page 16.

IRISH COFFEE

INGREDIENTS

2 teaspoons brown sugar, or to taste
120 ml strong, hot coffee
45 ml Irish whiskey
30 ml cream, lightly whipped

METHOD

Place sugar in an Irish coffee glass or a mug, then add coffee and stir until sugar has dissolved. Add Irish whiskey. Float cream by pouring it in slowly over the back of a spoon.

JUNGLE JUICE

INGREDIENTS
30 ml vodka
30 ml white rum
15 ml triple sec
30 ml cranberry juice
30 ml orange juice
30 ml pineapple juice
22.5 ml lime juice
7.5 ml grenadine
Garnish: orange slice

METHOD
Combine all ingredients in a cocktail shaker with ice. Shake until the outside of the cocktail shaker becomes frosted. Strain and pour into a Collins glass. Garnish.

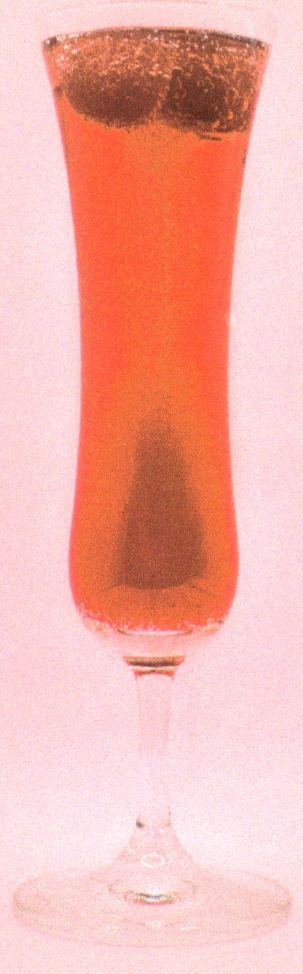

KIR ROYALE

INGREDIENTS
10 ml crème de cassis
90 ml sparkling wine
Garnish: raspberries or blackberries

METHOD
Pour crème de cassis into a champagne flute and top with sparkling wine. Garnish.

LEMON DROP

INGREDIENTS
45 ml citrus vodka
15 ml triple sec
20 ml lemon juice
5 ml sugar syrup
Garnish: lemon twist

METHOD
Combine all ingredients in a cocktail shaker with ice. Shake until the outside of the cocktail shaker becomes frosted. Strain and pour into a cocktail glass. Garnish.

Note: The recipe for sugar syrup is on page 17.

LOVE POTION #9

INGREDIENTS
45 ml vodka
15 ml peach schnapps
90 ml pink grapefruit juice
Garnish: strawberry

METHOD
Combine all ingredients in a cocktail shaker with ice. Shake until the outside of the cocktail shaker becomes frosted. Strain and pour into a cocktail glass. Garnish.

Note: Can be served with a sugar rim, see page 17.

MARGARITA

INGREDIENTS

FOR THE SALT RIM
lemon wedge
salt

COCKTAIL
40 ml tequila
25 ml Cointreau
20 ml lime juice
Garnish: lime slice

METHOD

Rim the edge of a cocktail glass with salt by wiping the edge with lemon wedge and then rolling the edge in salt. Combine all ingredients in a cocktail shaker with ice. Shake until the outside of the cocktail shaker becomes frosted. Strain and pour into the glass. Garnish.

MIDORI SOUR

INGREDIENTS
45 ml Midori
15 ml lemon juice
15 ml lime juice
soda water, to top
Garnish: lime slice and maraschino cherry

METHOD
Add Midori, lime juice and lemon juice to an old-fashioned glass filled with ice. Stir and top with soda water. Garnish.

MOJITO

INGREDIENTS
6 mint leaves
10 ml sugar syrup
30 ml lime juice
45 ml white rum
soda water, to top
Garnish: lime slice

METHOD
In a highball glass, muddle mint leaves with sugar syrup and lime juice to release the oils. Fill the glass with crushed ice and pour in rum. Top with soda water. Stir. Garnish.

Note: The recipe for sugar syrup is on page 17.

MUDSLIDE

INGREDIENTS
45 ml vodka
45 ml Irish cream
45 ml Tia Maria
70 ml cream
Garnish: shaved chocolate

METHOD
Combine all ingredients in a cocktail shaker with ice. Shake until the outside of the cocktail shaker becomes frosted. Strain and pour into a cocktail glass. Garnish.

MULLED WINE

Mulled wine can be made in smaller batches, but here it is made in a large batch rather than by the glass. Serves 4.

INGREDIENTS

750 ml dry red wine
125 ml brandy or orange liqueur
40 g sugar
1 orange, thinly sliced (also peeled, if you would like a less-bitter drink)
8 cloves
2 cinnamon sticks
2 star anise
Garnish: citrus slice, cinnamon stick, star anise

METHOD

Add all ingredients to a saucepan and stir to combine. Heat until just simmering – do not let the mixture bubble. Reduce heat to very low, cover and simmer for 30 minutes. Taste and add more sugar if required. Strain and pour into heatproof glasses or mugs. Garnish.

NAKED AND FAMOUS

INGREDIENTS
30 ml mezcal
30 ml Aperol
30 ml yellow Chartreuse
30 ml lime juice
Garnish: lime wedge

METHOD
Combine all ingredients in a cocktail shaker with ice. Shake until the outside of the cocktail shaker becomes frosted. Strain and pour into a cocktail glass. Garnish.

NUTTY SUMMER

INGREDIENTS

30 ml advocaat
15 ml Malibu rum
15 ml amaretto
15 ml pineapple juice
15 ml cream
Garnish: 3 dashes Angostura bitters

METHOD

Combine all ingredients in a cocktail shaker with ice. Shake until the outside of the cocktail shaker becomes frosted. Strain and pour into a cocktail glass. Garnish.

OLD FASHIONED

INGREDIENTS
12.5 ml sugar syrup
3 dashes Angostura bitters
60 ml bourbon, or any whiskey
Garnish: orange slice and maraschino cherry

METHOD
In an old-fashioned glass, muddle sugar syrup with Angostura bitters. Fill the glass with ice, add bourbon and stir. Garnish.

Note: The recipe for sugar syrup is on page 17.

PALOMA

INGREDIENTS
45 ml tequila
20 ml pink grapefruit juice
10 ml lime juice
7.5 ml agave syrup
90 ml pink grapefruit soda
Garnish: grapefruit wedge

METHOD
Combine tequila, pink grapefruit juice, lime juice and agave syrup in a cocktail shaker with ice. Shake until the outside of the cocktail shaker becomes frosted. Strain and pour into a Collins glass. Top with pink grapefruit soda. Garnish.

PERFECT STORM

INGREDIENTS
60 ml spiced rum
15 ml lime juice
2 dashes Angostura bitters
ginger beer, to top
Garnish: lime wedge

METHOD
Combine spiced rum, lime juice and Angostura bitters in a cocktail shaker with ice. Shake until the outside of the cocktail shaker becomes frosted. Strain and pour into a highball glass. Top with ginger beer. Garnish.

PIÑA COLADA

INGREDIENTS
60 ml Malibu
120 ml pineapple juice
60 ml coconut cream
Garnish: pineapple chunk and maraschino cherry

METHOD
Combine all ingredients in a cocktail shaker with ice. Shake until the outside of the cocktail shaker becomes frosted. Strain and pour into a hurricane glass. Garnish.

PORN STAR MARTINI

INGREDIENTS
45 ml vanilla vodka
15 ml Passoã
30 ml passionfruit puree
15 ml lime juice
15 ml sugar syrup
60 ml prosecco
Garnish: 1/2 passionfruit

METHOD
Combine vanilla vodka, Passoã, passionfruit puree, lime juice and sugar syrup in a cocktail shaker with ice. Shake until the outside of the cocktail shaker becomes frosted. Strain and pour into a cocktail glass. Garnish. Pour prosecco into a shot glass and serve on the side.

Note: The recipe for sugar syrup is on page 17.

QUARANTINI

INGREDIENTS
45 ml gin
30 ml Cointreau
30 ml cranberry juice
15 ml apple juice
sparkling wine, to top
Garnish: lime twist

METHOD
Combine gin, Cointreau, cranberry juice and apple juice in a cocktail shaker with ice. Shake until the outside of the cocktail shaker becomes frosted. Strain and pour into a cocktail glass. Top with sparkling wine. Garnish.

RUSTY NAIL

INGREDIENTS
60 ml Scotch whisky
22.5 ml Drambuie
Garnish: lemon peel

METHOD
Add ingredients in any order to an old-fashioned glass filled with ice. Stir. Garnish.

SANGRIA

Sangria is always made for a crowd. Serves 4–5.

INGREDIENTS

750 ml dry red wine
125 ml brandy
200 ml orange juice
40 g brown sugar
mix of fruit (apples, oranges, grapes, strawberries), cut into small pieces

METHOD

In a large pitcher, combine liquids and sugar, then stir in fruit. Refrigerate for at least 2 hours before serving in stemless wine glasses or tumblers.

SCREWDRIVER

INGREDIENTS
60 ml vodka
90 ml orange juice

METHOD
Fill a Collins glass with ice.
Pour in the vodka, then the
orange juice.

SEX ON THE BEACH

INGREDIENTS
45 ml vodka
15 ml peach schnapps
45 ml orange juice
45 ml cranberry juice
Garnish: orange slice and maraschino cherry

METHOD
Combine vodka, peach schnapps and orange juice in a cocktail shaker with ice. Shake until the outside of the cocktail shaker becomes frosted. Strain into a highball glass filled with ice. Top with cranberry juice. Garnish.

SIDECAR

INGREDIENTS

FOR THE SUGAR RIM
lemon wedge
sugar

COCKTAIL
50 ml cognac
30 ml Cointreau
20 ml lemon juice

METHOD
Wipe the rim of a cocktail glass with lemon wedge, then roll the rim in sugar. Set aside to dry. Combine cognac, Cointreau and lemon juice in a cocktail shaker with ice. Shake until the outside of the cocktail shaker becomes frosted. Strain into the sugar-rimmed glass.

SIX CYLINDER

INGREDIENTS
15 ml gin
15 ml cherry brandy
15 ml Campari
15 ml sweet vermouth
15 ml dry vermouth
15 ml Dubonnet
Garnish: lemon peel

METHOD
Combine all ingredients in a mixing glass filled with ice. Stir. Strain and pour into a cocktail glass. Garnish.

SUFFERING BASTARD

INGREDIENTS

30 ml bourbon
30 ml dry gin
5 ml lime juice
dash of Angostura bitters
ginger beer, to top
Garnish: orange slice and mint sprig

METHOD

Combine bourbon, gin, lime juice and Angostura bitters in a cocktail shaker with ice. Shake until the outside of the cocktail shaker becomes frosted. Strain and pour into a Collins glass. Top with ginger beer. Garnish.

SUNFLOWER

INGREDIENTS

absinthe, to rinse
30 ml gin
30 ml Cointreau
30 ml elderflower liqueur
30 ml lemon juice
Garnish: lemon twist or edible flower

METHOD

Rinse the inside of a cocktail glass with absinthe, then discard the excess and set the glass aside. Combine remaining ingredients in a cocktail shaker with ice. Shake until the outside of the cocktail shaker becomes frosted. Strain and pour into the prepared glass. Garnish.

SWAMP THING

INGREDIENTS
2 slices cucumber, 1 cm thick, peeled
15 ml sugar syrup
60 ml gold rum
30 ml absinthe
15 ml lime juice

METHOD
In a cocktail shaker, muddle cucumber with sugar syrup to yield as much juice as possible. Add remaining ingredients with ice. Shake until the outside of the cocktail shaker becomes frosted. Strain and pour into a cocktail glass.

Note: The recipe for sugar syrup is on page 17.

TEQUILA SUNRISE

INGREDIENTS
45 ml tequila
125 ml orange juice
15 ml grenadine
Garnish: orange slice and maraschino cherry

METHOD
Fill a Collins glass with ice. Pour over tequila and top with orange juice. Pour grenadine into centre so it sinks to the bottom. Garnish.

TEQUILA SUNSET

The Tequila Sunset is the same as the Tequila Sunrise except for the amount of tequila added.

INGREDIENTS
60 ml tequila
125 ml orange juice
15 ml grenadine
Garnish: orange slice and maraschino cherry

METHOD
Fill a Collins glass with ice. Pour over tequila and top with orange juice. Pour grenadine into centre of glass. Garnish.

VIOLET FIZZ

INGREDIENTS
45 ml Old Tom Gin
7.5 ml crème de violette
30 ml lemon juice
15 ml sugar syrup
30 ml cream
15 ml egg white
soda water, to top
Garnish: lemon twist or a violet

METHOD
Combine gin, crème de violette, lemon juice, sugar syrup, cream and egg white in a cocktail shaker without ice (shaking without ice changes the egg white consistency and creates foam). Add ice and shake again until the outside of the cocktail shaker becomes frosted. Strain and pour into a Collins glass. Top with soda water. Garnish.

Note: The recipe for sugar syrup is on page 17.

WHISKEY SOUR

INGREDIENTS

50 ml bourbon
25 ml lemon juice
15 ml sugar syrup
15 ml egg white
Garnish: orange wedge or orange slice and maraschino cherry

METHOD

Combine all ingredients in a cocktail shaker without ice (shaking without ice changes the egg white consistency and creates foam). Add ice and shake again until the outside of the cocktail shaker becomes frosted. Strain and pour into an old-fashioned glass filled with ice. Garnish.

Note: The recipe for sugar syrup is on page 17.

WHITE RUSSIAN

INGREDIENTS
45 ml Kahlúa
45 ml vodka
30 ml cream

METHOD
Fill an old-fashioned glass with ice, then pour in Kahlúa and vodka. Stir, then add cream.

WHOA, NELLIE!

INGREDIENTS

45 ml rye whiskey
25 ml dark rum
25 ml orange liqueur
15 ml grapefruit juice
15 ml lemon juice
15 ml sugar syrup

METHOD

Combine all ingredients in a cocktail shaker with ice. Shake until the outside of the cocktail shaker becomes frosted. Strain and pour into a cocktail glass.

Note: The recipe for sugar syrup is on page 17.

WOO WOO

INGREDIENTS
50 ml vodka
25 ml peach schnapps
100 ml cranberry juice
2.5 ml lime juice
Garnish: lime slice

METHOD
Combine all ingredients
in a cocktail shaker with ice.
Shake until the outside of the
cocktail shaker becomes frosted.
Strain and pour into a
Collins glass. Garnish.

ZOMBIE

INGREDIENTS

45 ml white rum
30 ml Jamaican rum
20 ml overproof rum
15 ml falernum liqueur
30 ml pineapple juice
20 ml lime juice
10 ml pink grapefruit juice
dash of grenadine

Garnish: orange wedge, mint leaves and maraschino cherry

METHOD

Combine all ingredients in a cocktail shaker with ice. Shake until the outside of the cocktail shaker becomes frosted. Strain and pour into a hurricane glass filled with ice.

DRINK FINDER

Absinthe
  Absinthe Drip 20
  Comfortably Numb 34
  Eye Opener 41
  Sunflower 81
  Swamp Thing 82
Advocaat
  Fluffy Duck 42
  Nutty Summer 67
Amaretto
  Eternal Spirit 40
  Eye Opener 41
  Godfather 47
  Godmother 48
  Nutty Summer 67
Aperol
  Aperol Spritz 22
  Naked and Famous 66
Bacardi
  see Rum
Bourbon
  Old Fashioned 68
  Suffering Bastard 80
  Whiskey Sour 86

Brandy
  Brandy Alexander 31
  Mulled Wine 64
  Sangria 75
  Six Cylinder 79
Calvados
  Corpse Reviver 35
Campari
  Six Cylinder 79
Champagne and wine
  Aperol Spritz 22
  Bellini 26
  Champagne Cocktail 33
  French 75 43
  Kir Royale 57
  Mulled Wine 64
  Porn Star Martini 72
  Quarantini 73
  Sangria 75
Chartreuse
  Green With Envy 51
  Naked and Famous 66

Chocolate liqueur
  Brandy Alexander 31
  Death by Chocolate 36
  Grasshopper 49
Coffee liqueur
  Baby Guiness 24
  Black Russian 28
  Mudslide 63
  White Russian 87
Cognac
  Between the Sheets 27
  Champagne Cocktail 33
  Corpse Reviver 35
  Sidecar 78
Cointreau
  see Orange-flavoured liqueur
Crème de cacao
  see Chocolate liqueur
Crème de cassis
  El Diablo 37
  Kir Royale 57

Crème de menthe
   Grasshopper **49**

Crème de Mûre
   Bramble **30**

Crème de violette
   Violet Fizz **85**

Curaçao, blue or orange
   see Orange-flavoured liqueur

Drambuie
   Rusty Nail **74**

Dubonnet
   Six Cylinder **79**

Elderflower liqueur
   Green Goddess **50**
   Sunflower **81**

Falernum liqueur
   Zombie **90**

Fernet-Branca
   Hanky Panky **52**

Gin
   Bee's Knees **25**
   Bramble **30**
   Breakfast Martini **32**
   Fluffy Duck **42**
   French 75 **43**
   Gin and Tonic **45**
   Gin Basil Smash **46**
   Green Goddess **50**
   Green With Envy **51**
   Hanky Panky **52**
   Quarantini **73**
   Six Cylinder **79**
   Suffering Bastard **80**
   Sunflower **81**
   Violet Fizz **85**

Irish Cream
   Baby Guiness **24**
   Mudslide **63**

Kahlúa
   see Coffee liqueur

Malibu
   see Rum

Mezcal
   see Tequila

Midori
   Midori Sour **61**

Orange-flavoured liqueur (Cointreau, triple sec and curaçao)
   Between the Sheets **27**
   Breakfast Martini **32**
   Comfortably Numb **34**
   El Presidente **38**
   Eye Opener **41**
   Esse Emme **39**
   Fluffy Duck **42**
   Jungle Juice **56**
   Lemon Drop **58**
   Margarita **60**
   Mulled Wine **64**
   Quarantini **73**
   Sidecar **78**
   Sunflower **81**
   Whoa, Nellie! **88**

Passoa
   Porn Star Martini **72**

Parfait d'amour
   Esse Emme **39**

Peach Schnapps
   Esse Emme **39**
   Fuzzy Navel **44**
   High Voltage **53**
   Love Potion #9 **59**
   Sex on the Beach **77**
   Woo Woo **89**

Pimento dram
   Comfortably Numb **34**

Port
   Astral Plane **23**

Prosecco
  see Champagne and wine
Rum
  Air Mail 21
  Between the Sheets 27
  El Presidente 38
  Eternal Spirit 40
  Eye Opener 41
  Honey Bee 54
  Jungle Juice 56
  Mojito 62
  Nutty Summer 67
  Perfect Storm 70
  Piña Colada 71
  Rum Fluffy Duck 42
  Swamp Thing 82
  Whoa, Nellie! 88
  Zombie 90
Salers Gentiane
  Astral Plane 23
Schnapps, Peach
  see Peach schnapps
Southern Comfort
  Comfortably Numb 34
Tequila
  El Diablo 37
  High Voltage 53
  Margarita 60
  Naked and Famous 66
  Paloma 69
  Tequila Sunrise 83
  Tequila Sunset 84
Tia Maria
  see Coffee liqueur
Triple Sec
  see Orange-flavoured liqueur
Vermouth
  Corpse Reviver 35
  El Presidente 38
  Eternal Spirit 40
  Hanky Panky 52
  Six Cylinder 79
Vodka
  Black Russian 28
  Bloody Mary 29
  Death by Chocolate 36
  Esse Emme 39
  Hairy Navel
  Godmother 48
  Jungle Juice 56
  Lemon Drop 58
  Love Potion #9 59
  Mudslide 63
  Porn Star Martini 72
  Screwdriver 76
  Sex on the Beach 77
  White Russian 87
  Woo Woo 89
Whisk(e)y
  Godfather 47
  Irish Coffee 55
  Old Fashioned 68
  Rusty Nail 74
  Whiskey Sour 86
  Whoa, Nellie! 88

ACKNOWLEDGEMENTS

Many thanks to everyone who patiently listened and offered support when I spoke to them about my cocktail project over the past three years. You know who you are. Also thank you to everyone who has been involved with the editing and production, with a special shout-out to Julie Richards who must have seen several versions of this project over different stages and Katie Purvis for the final edit. Thanks to Lorna Hendry for the typesetting and design, and as always a big shoutout to my family and writing-crew friends who are always there to keep me going, no matter what crazy ideas I come up with.

www.ingramcontent.com/pod-product-compliance
Lightning Source LLC
Chambersburg PA
CBHW061757290426
44109CB00030B/2885